I0458625

WISEBLOOD ESSAYS IN CONTEMPORARY CULTURE NO. 18

THE
WAYWARD
THOMIST

A Critical Introduction to
John Martin Finlay

JAMES MATTHEW WILSON

WISEBLOOD BOOKS
2025

COPYRIGHT © 2025 WISEBLOOD BOOKS

All rights reserved, including the right to reproduce this book or any portions thereof in any form whatsoever except for brief quotations in book reviews. For information, address the publisher:

WISEBLOOD BOOKS
Joshua Hren, Editor-in-Chief
Post Office Box 870
Menomonee Falls, WI 53052
www.wisebloodbooks.com

Printed in the United States of America

ISBN: 978-1-963319-85-9

For David Middleton

Writing from the family farm in Enterprise, Alabama, to the literary critic and *Southern Review* editor Lewis P. Simpson, the already doomed poet John Martin Finlay paused a moment to reflect on cattle. "I can't help but like the cows," he told Simpson, "they are good Thomistic animals and save one from the madness of Berkeley."[1]

Over the course of the two decades before he wrote those words, Finlay (1941-1991), through natural talent, single-minded but wayward determination, and the goodwill of others, had all but remade himself into his own pious ideal of the poet and man of letters. That ideal was itself modeled on two exemplars, the poets and critics Allen Tate and Yvor Winters. Both writers were two generations older than Finlay and had given shape to the late modernist period (1930-1960) in American literature. The first was a southern agrarian, a literary critic, a poet of tense, obscure lyrics, and, importantly, a Catholic convert. The second was an equally wide-ranging critic, a professor at Stanford University, a poet of classical clarity and severe judgment, and a non-Christian intellectual theist who accepted Thomas Aquinas as his philosophical master. Finlay would follow them as closely as Dante followed Virgil, becoming a poet of the American South like Tate, an intellectualist in philosophy on roughly the model of Aquinas and Winters, a defender of classical humanism like both of the poets, and, finally a convert to the Catholic

---

1. John Martin Finlay, *The Collected Poems of John Martin Finlay*, ed. David Middleton and John P. Doucet (Belmont, NC: Wiseblood Books, 2020), 221.

Church, in communion with which he spent the last, fruitful, but agonizing, decade of his life.

Drawing on the work of Tate and Winters, Finlay would compose a slender body of poems and a no less lean body of literary and philosophical prose, all of which sought to understand and critique the "Gnosticism" of the modern age and to arrive at a clear, rational understanding of human nature and the goodness of being. He strained himself to drive away the madness of Berkeley and of others he called gnostics, while straining no less to envision in his poetry a way of dwelling in the world as solid, content, and good as that of the farmyard cows. Finlay's work was unfashionable and largely overlooked in his lifetime; even so, it made a modest but worthy contribution to the American literary culture of the twentieth century, and it merits renewed attention in our day.

Finlay the man lived a disordered but heroic life, as he fought the desires of the flesh and sought, with the help of Aquinas, to redeem both mind and blood, body and soul, and, as it were, to live like a "good Thomistic animal." The stakes of that quest were made all the more grave by the AIDS virus, a disease that Finlay contracted, somewhere in the bathhouses of New Orleans, when it was still a terrible mystery being reported in the newspapers. The disease would cut off his life; the disease also would focus his mind on a true understanding of what it means to be a "rational animal," a composite of intellectual soul and material body. Mind and blood (the title of the first edition of his collected poems) belong together; they constitute us as one human being, a composite whole; and yet, for so many persons, ancient and modern, they pull against each other and tear the human animal apart.

The Influence of Tate and Winters

Allen Tate had first risen to fame as a member of the Fugitive poets at Vanderbilt University in the 1920s. Along with his professor and fellow Fugitive, John Crowe Ransom, Tate (1899-1979) helped to establish an ironic, dense, impersonal, and formally taut mode of lyric poetry as the predominant style of the period. Also in concert with Ransom, Tate later helped rally a group of writers to declare themselves the Southern Agrarians and to launch an entirely literary campaign against the incursion of a "northern" industrial economy and its advocate, the chamber of commerce, into southern life. The agrarians first announced themselves with the volume *I'll Take My Stand* in 1930.[2] Tate's essay stood apart from the others in the volume in one crucial respect. It defended the "feudal," agrarian traditions of the South, but somewhat obliquely argued that the South's great cultural weakness had been its failure to embrace the suitably "feudal" religion of Catholicism. Most of the Agrarians saw the need for "religion" as a dimension of culture; Tate viewed Catholicism proper as foundational. This was among the first indications that Tate, who excelled at identifying the weaknesses of modern

2. Twelve Southerners, *I'll Take My Stand: The South and the Agrarian Tradition* (Baton Rouge: Louisiana State University Press, 1977).

culture, would find the solution to those weaknesses in the Catholic Church—to which he converted in 1950.

Ransom and Tate would further collaborate in establishing the academic literary culture of the period. By the time Ransom published his book *The New Criticism* in 1941, the academic study of literature was already in the process of establishing as its standard the close reading of literary texts with minimal attention to their historical and biographical sources.[3] These practices would later be dismissed as ahistorical, superficial, and ideological, but they were in fact among the first and most successful efforts to join aesthetic appreciation and academic rigor to the contemplative and religious dimensions proper to the intellectual life. Literary study took on some of the purpose that philosophy and theology had long served, as humanizing but also difficult pursuits. In his twenties, Finlay met in person both Ransom and fellow Agrarian writer Andrew Lytle, but it was the figure of Tate that held his imagination. This must have been due in part to the religious character of Tate's life and work. Finlay was always a confessing Christian, but his conversion to Catholicism came about through an intellectual sense of the Church's necessity that resembled Tate's. The Church was the answer to the reductive rationalism and disorder of the modern age. It alone could teach us to reconcile mind and blood.

Finlay met Tate twice in 1966, including when the older poet visited the University of Alabama, Tuscaloosa, where Finlay completed his bachelor's and then master's

3. John Crowe Ransom, *The New Criticism* (New York: New Directions, 1941).

degrees in English literature. Finlay was probably behind the invitation; he was photographed with Tate and introduced him from the podium, quoting Lytle in observing that "Mr Tate's theme is nothing more or less than what is left of Christendom."[4] That same year, Finlay wrote to Tate to say that Tate's poems "are so much a part of me, have helped me to see so much of my own life that I cannot imagine what I would be without them."[5] In his copy of Tate's *Collected Essays*, he inscribed an epigram to the poet who had helped "our now lean language" to "sing / Of laurel and the rough dogwood / Caught in the single glow of faith."[6] At the most general level, Tate's southern origins and concerns were what inspired Finlay. Finlay was raised on the family farm and sympathized emotionally with the agrarian ethic even as he sought to escape living it; he found the "reactionary" attitudes of Tate appealing.[7] Despite his testimony to Tate himself, Finlay thought Tate's poems difficult to comprehend, as indeed have most people; but, he surely appreciated the appearance of classical austerity and rich patterns of allusion and symbol in Tate's work. To speak, as Finlay does, of "lean language," is to voice praise, not to suggest impoverishment.[8]

---

4. Finlay, *The Collected Poems*, 197.

5. Finlay, *The Collected Poems*, 192.

6. Finlay, *The Collected Poems*, 196.

7. Allen Tate, *Reactionary Essays on Poetry and Ideas* (United Kingdom: C. Scribner's & Sons, 1936).

8. As in "Audubon at Oakley" in *The Collected Poems*, 28.

In the epigram quoted just above, he also speaks of "Salty Aeneas" coming "to Rome."[9] This alludes to the southern mythos in which the Old South is the heir of ancient Troy, noble in its defeat by the pillaging "Greeks" of the Union army. In two of Tate's best poems he would deploy that familiar trope to critique modern America. We should also note, whenever Finlay uses the word "salt" in a poem (as he does far more often than he should), it is a term of praise. Among salt's connotations, for Finlay as for the Elizabethan epigram tradition he is following, are its suggestions of the intellectual, classical, and austere. Salt, for Finlay, was a property he found in Winters and Tate alike: an acerbic vision that sees into the essence of things, sometimes for the sake of satire, and sometimes for the sake of austere moral judgment. Salt is the antidote to the sugar of romantic sentimentalism; it is the quality of a poetry of the mind, at once plain and intelligent. In "The History of a Traditionalist," written about Winters's disciple, J. V. Cunningham, Finlay writes,

> He learned what tougher masters can impart
> The salt and muscle of that English art
> Before crazed adolescents wrecked its mind.
> He took the meat out of the antique rind
> And never aped mere manners from the past.[10]

While the portrait is specifically of Cunningham, it illustrates characteristics that Finlay admired in Tate and

9. Finlay, *The Collected Poems*, 196.

10. Finlay, *The Collected Poems*, 70.

Winters as well: a poetry of "muscle," meaning hard-headed reason, and "salt," a perceptiveness that sees through our "crazed" romantic fantasies. Such poetry nourishes itself on the tradition, but with its "meat," its inner essence, rather than its superficial style or "manners."

One of Tate's better-known poems, and one Finlay claimed to have memorized, was a meditative lyric written during a fellowship in Europe, "The Mediterranean." The only period during which Finlay lived outside his native Alabama and Louisiana, where he completed his doctorate over the decade of the 1970s, was an abortive residency on the Greek island of Corfu and, later, in Paris. Tate thus provided Finlay a model of the southern poet as at once rooted and universal, provincial and cosmopolitan, a poet for whom the South was a modern American heir to the ancient cultural traditions of the West.

Profound though Tate's influence was, it pales in comparison to that of the California poet and critic Yvor Winters (1900-1968). "What I owe Yvor Winters," Finlay would record: "Nearly everything."[11] Finlay's habits were spectacular in their carelessness and disorder. More than one of the biographical accounts of Finlay report his tendency to sit up into the early hours talking, smoking, and drinking whiskey.[12] During his college years, he allowed a "small mountain of cigarette butts" to pile on "the floor of his VW bug as he drove some 40,000 miles without

11. Jeffrey Goodman, "The Romance of Modern Classicism: Remarks on the Life and Work of John Finlay, 1941-1991," *Alabama Literary Review*, 14.2 (Fall 2000): 34.

12. Goodman, "The Romance of Modern Classicism," 31.

changing the oil."[13] During an early stint teaching at Alabama College, he made a practice of mooching alcohol, supper, and the use of a television—which invention he professed to disdain—off Loretta and Bill Cobb. Bill was a colleague, and Finlay lived in the apartment upstairs from the couple.[14] His teaching often suffered after late nights drinking Scotch at the Cobbs'. The Cobbs were once—and only once—invited to lunch at Finlay's apartment as an act of gratitude. They arrived to discover "canned tomato soup . . . boiling volcanically on the stove" and, in the refrigerator, "only a six-pack of beer and a carton of cigarettes."[15] Finlay, in brief, was a mess.

In perfect contrast to Finlay's slovenly ways, Winters was the great practitioner of classical discipline and restraint. According to Winters's distinguished early essay, "The Morality of Poetry," the "Spiritual control in a poem . . . is simply a manifestation of the spiritual control within the poet"; it was "an important means by which the poet arrived at a realization of spiritual control."[16] He elaborates that his "is a conception of poetry as a technique of contemplation, of comprehension, a technique which does not eliminate the need for philosophy or religion, but which, rather, completes and enriches them."[17]

13. Goodman, "The Romance of Modern Classicism," 33.

14. Goodman, "The Romance of Modern Classicism," 34.

15. Goodman, "The Romance of Modern Classicism," 35.

16. Yvor Winters, *In Defense of Reason* (Denver, CO: University of Denver Press, 1947), 21.

17. Winters, *In Defense of Reason*, 21-22.

The aesthetic contemplation of the poet concentrated the mind and moved it toward the classical ideal of self-mastery. And so, Winters concludes, it "should offer a means of enriching one's awareness of human experience and of so rendering greater the possibility of intelligence in the course of future action."[18] Poetry is at once a form to be contemplated, a way of knowing reality, a means to order, and a guide to living. Finlay's discovery of Winters was not mere fascination with an artist but an encounter with a tough-minded writer with the intellectual theory and substance to discipline and reform his own flailing, haphazard existence.

In the late 1960s, Finlay wrote to Donald E. Stanford, at Louisiana State University, sending him some of his poems and, eventually, requesting admission to the doctoral program.[19] Stanford had been one of Winters's many acolytes in Palo Alto. Winters had published and praised his early poems. Stanford's literary criticism followed the interests (Robert Bridges) and the judgments (admiring Wallace Stevens, condemning T. S. Eliot) of his master. At LSU he edited *The Southern Review*, through which office he would help to establish Finlay's modest career as poet and critic.

During his years in Baton Rouge, Finlay befriended the poets Lindon Stall, Wyatt Prunty, and David Middleton, the last of whom now serves as Finlay's literary executor and has been the chief agent of Finlay's posthumous

18. Winters, *In Defense of Reason*, 29.

19. Goodman, "The Romance of Modern Classicism," 36-38.

reputation. All the poets except Stall stood athwart the rise of the Beat and New York School poets and, under Winters's and Stanford's influence, continued the practice of metrical verse in a classical plain style.[20] Over the course of a decade, interrupted only by his extended European travels, Finlay worked on his dissertation, "The Unfleshed Eye: A Study of Intellectual Theism in the Poetry of Yvor Winters."[21]

ILL TIMED

By 1980, the now forty-year-old Finlay had written at least a handful of published poems and a work of significant scholarship. He was known to a few eminent writers and had a sympathetic circle of contemporaries. This was not insignificant, but it also was not much for a man on the brink of middle age. Rather than seek an academic appointment, he returned to the family farm—not out of agrarian sentiment, but in order to secure the freedom to write the poems and essays he hoped, eventually, would win him a university post and a reputation. Had he been born two decades sooner, Finlay would assuredly have succeeded in this aim, but the hour was much too late and for two reasons.

---

20. Goodman, "The Romance of Modern Classicism," 36.

21. John Martin Finlay, "The Unfleshed Eye: A Study of Intellectual Theism in the Poetry and Criticism of Yvor Winters" (PhD Diss., Lousiana State University, 1980).

In the years when Finlay first discovered their work, Tate and Winters had attained formidable reputations among the American men of letters of their age. Both had received extensive public recognition, including the Bollingen prize (Tate in 1956, Winters in 1960). But American culture was entering a time not only of swift transition but of serious tumult. By the time Finlay finished his doctorate, Tate and Winters were dead and their reputations in swift decline. Among the readers of *The Southern Review*, and in the halls of the Stanford English Department and a few other outposts, they remained defining figures, to be sure, and Winters's former students continued to earn well-deserved, if small, reputations as contrarian classicists in a formless and demotic age. But an era had passed.

Tate had died just the year before Finlay completed his doctorate. *Poetry* magazine honored him with an issue that included one of Tate's last lectures, "Mere Literature and the Lost Traveller."[22] This lecture would influence nearly all of Finlay's work thereafter, as we shall see, but to today's reader it sounds more like a valediction, an ambling discussion on a well-rehearsed theme from an earlier epoch. Other figures touched by the influence of Tate and Winters, but of an earlier generation, including the poets Robert Lowell, Richard Wilbur, and Anthony Hecht—all born between 1917 and 1923—enjoyed prominence and prestige throughout their careers. Even so, they

---

22. Allen Tate, "Mere Literature and the Lost Traveller [sic]," *Poetry*, 135.2 (November 1979), 93-102.

were already deemed out of step with the literary spirit of the age. Finlay synthesized the two master poets' qualities but did so too late for it to earn him similar attention, much less either acclaim or criticism.[23] He was known to a small circle of distinguished writers, but these same writers were themselves largely, like Winters before them, "master[s] obscured by history."[24]

There is still another reason, and one of even greater consequence, to speak of Finlay's life and work as ill-timed. Over the course of many years, Finlay had secretly been visiting "the backrooms of gay bars and baths" in New Orleans.[25] He understood these proclivities as a "demon" of the blood, over which he sought to gain control by means of the reason of the mind. "I can't sleep," he recorded in his notebook on June 5, 1980: "As soon as I turn the lights out, the demon . . . comes out . . . how many times I have performed exactly his bidding."[26] After succumbing to the demon, he would bow in prayer and seek forgiveness. In the year of this notebook entry, Finlay followed Tate into the Catholic Church. By this time, however, the demon had claimed a mortal victory. As news first spread of the AIDS virus at the start of the new decade, Finlay

---

23. Finlay, *The Collected Poems*, 195.

24. Quoted in Elizabeth Isaacs, *An Introduction to the Poetry of Yvor Winters* (Athens, OH: Swallow Press, 1981), xiv.

25. Goodman, "The Romance of Modern Classicism," 42.

26. John Martin Finlay, *The Collected Prose of John Martin Finlay*, ed. David Middleton and John P. Doucet (Belmont, NC: Wiseblood Books, 2020), 323.

already sensed he had contracted it. In this he was correct. His retreat to Alabama enabled him to work in freedom, but also to conceal the consequences of the disease from others. By 1988, his symptoms were visible, as became clear during one of his few moments of public recognition. The poets Dick Davis and Edgar Bowers, both associated with the Winters circle, invited Finlay to read at the University of California, Santa Barbara. By then, he was "pale ... dizzy and nauseated."[27] In the year ahead, he would lie bedridden in the living room of the family home, become incontinent, and, soon, go blind. In the last months before his death he was too weak to hold a telephone to his ear. He dictated his last and greatest poem, "A Prayer to the Father," to his sister. He died February 17, 1991.

The Demon and the Incarnation

Finlay's private struggle with sexual desire provides a point of entry into the great moral and literary themes of his work, an entry aptly labeled in the title of his posthumous collected poems, *Mind and Blood*.[28] Those themes take their point of departure from Winters and also from Tate. Finlay followed Winters in his conviction that the discipline of the poetic art was a means of establishing rational order or self-mastery in the soul. Through Winters, he discovered the work of Thomas Aquinas and the great scholastic's distinctions between faith and reason,

27. Goodman, "The Romance of Classicism," 45.

28. Finlay, *The Collected Poems*, 7.

nature and grace, as well as his existential metaphysics of the goodness of being. As Finlay observed in his dissertation and in the short excerpt from it that was collected in his first and only completed book of essays, Winters embraced Aquinas's respect for natural reason, but did not share Aquinas's affirmation of the goodness of being in general.

In this, Finlay was largely correct. The young Winters, influenced by Ralph Waldo Emerson, had fantasized in his poems about communion with nature as a kind of self-annihilation, a dissolving of the rational soul and a merging with the wildness of material being. In Winters's "Two Songs of Advent," for instance, the desert landscape appears as an alien and lonely reality, but then the very foreign spirit of nature takes possession of us: "Listen! Listen! I enter now your thought."[29] Such an invasion and dissolution of the soul was not to be avoided, however, but to be cultivated. It was a romantic ecstasy at once terrible and compelling and, in principle, self-annihilating. Winters described it as a kind of solipsism which, because the self has merged with the wildness of nature, is also a monism. We see this in the final lines of "Alone":

> My own eyes did not exist!
> When I struck I never missed!
> Noon, felt and far away,
> My brain is a thousand bees.[30]

---

29. Yvor Winters, *The Poetry of Yvor Winters* (Chicago: Swallow Press, 1978), 19.

30. Winters, *The Poetry of Yvor Winters*, 94.

The self, at least for a moment, disappears and yet is everywhere. All that was far away is also interior to the self, hived in the self. The self is no longer a being, separate from nature, but wholly identical with it, such that its actions toward nature cannot fail, because the subject acting is one with the object.

An early experience of madness, while captive in the snow-covered solitude of the Rockies, led Winters to rethink the attraction of this self-dissolving kind of ecstasy.[31] He recorded the experience in his one published short story, "The Brink of Darkness," where he speaks of himself as "disturbed, uncentered, and finally obsessed as by an insidious power," as if subject to "a deliberate and malevolent invasion" by an "Eastern demon."[32] Eastern, he notes, because associated with the monism of Oriental thought that inspired, first, the German romantics and, second, Emerson's derivative philosophy of nature.

The experience changed Winters and his entire course in life. The cultivation of immersion in the oneness of nature ceased to be a romantic ideal and gradually came to appear as a madness to be avoided. He trained his sights on Emerson as exemplary of all those who would mislead human beings by enticing them to surrender their reason and their souls. In his critical work, Winters condemned Emerson and other romantics for their privileging of emotion over reason and their naïve assumption that man's "impulses" were naturally "good" and should be followed

---

31. Isaacs, *Introduction to the Poetry of Yvor Winters*, xii.

32. Winters, *The Poetry of Yvor Winters*, 223.

in a spirit of "automatism."[33] He would prosecute the case repeatedly in the course of his career, but never so fiercely as in a late pamphlet, where he lays at Emerson's feet (and at the feet of the unserious mediocrities who teach Emerson's work in the schools) responsibility for the death by suicide of Winters's sometime friend and fellow poet, the neo-romantic Hart Crane.[34]

Finlay concurred entirely with Winters's defense of the rational soul against emotional invasion, and he shared Winters's conviction that natural reason was sufficient to know the existence of God and to deduce the proper form of moral life from that knowledge.[35] But Finlay departed from Winters insofar as the older poet denied the goodness of natural being. Winters came to view nature itself as the demonic, malevolent presence always threatening to dissolve the soul. The sensuous delights of nature were a desirable good only if mastered; many human beings succumbed to this craving for the material and became themselves mere matter, robbed of the distinctly human principle of reason. As Finlay argued, Winters saw "a death-principle in the physical world."[36] Finlay, of course, knew the reality of the demon, but he refused to attribute

33. Winters, *In Defense of Reason*, 8.

34. Winters, *In Defense of Reason*, 577-603.

35. Finlay even discussed these matters with Winters's widow, Janet Lewis, to whom he gives a richer account of Aquinas's five ways of knowing God than Winters had provided (See, Winters, *In Defense of Reason*, 14 and Finlay, *The Collected Poems*, 201).

36. Finlay, *The Collected Prose*, 126.

personal demons to the wholeness of natural being. This, in language we have already noted, Finlay attributed to a gnostic and "Platonic" dimension in Winters thought which must be rejected.[37]

Winters admired Thomas Aquinas and had been substantially influenced by the French neo-Thomist philosopher and historian Etienne Gilson, but chiefly in terms of Aquinas's and Gilson's defense of philosophical reason. Winters knew Gilson's account of right reason in *The Unity of Philosophical Experience*, but seems not to have read the philosopher's classic of existential metaphysics, *Being and Some Philosophers*.[38] Finlay, in contrast, saw in Gilson's existential Thomism an explanation for Winters's failure to affirm the goodness of being. For Winters, only the essence of the disembodied and spiritual mind—whether that of the individual human, or the divine mind of the Creator God—could be affirmed as good. Aquinas, as Gilson described him, was concerned not merely with essence but with existence—and above all, with real being in its act of existing *as good*. Finlay thus convicts Winters with Gilson's own coinage as guilty of "existential neutrality," and of viewing the "flesh" as a mere "breeding ground of error and imperceptions."[39]

Insofar as Winters defended the good of the self-mastery of the soul and viewed the soul as ordered to the God

---

37. Finlay, *The Collected Prose*, 124.

38. See, James Matthew Wilson, "The Realism of Helen Pinkerton," *Christianity and Literature* 58.1 (Fall 2009): 629-652.

39. Finlay, *The Collected Prose*, 122-123.

whom reason could know as Being Itself, Finlay followed him. But Finlay knew from experience that, although the sins of the flesh may indicate the fallen condition of nature, they nonetheless were no indication that the flesh itself, that nature itself, is evil. Winters's solution to the malevolent demon of nature was, in a modification of classical stoicism, to accept the tragic reality of life in the world and to withdraw from it insofar as was necessary for the good of the rational mind. "Nor is the mind in vain," wrote Winters, in a poem celebrating the intellectual retreat of the scholar as a noble way of life.[40]

Finlay, in contrast, although he well knew the demon to which the flesh was prey, saw also the necessity for, and possibility of, a life of the body properly ordered and governed by reason. The good life could not be restricted to the interior of the mind but must suffuse the whole existence of the person. As Aquinas had argued in his non-dualistic and realistic account of being, the human being is composite, with the soul as the very form and act of the body.[41] If the soul's form extends to and actuates the body, so must it be possible for the goodness of the rational soul to inform the life of the body. Finlay's regret over his own aberrations did not lead him to condemn the life of the body but to yearn for one that was not destructive of the soul. This indeed became one of the most cogent themes of the poems he wrote in the last decade of his life.

---

40. Winters, *The Poetry of Yvor Winters*, 124.

41. Saint Thomas Aquinas, *Summa Theologica* I.75-76, trans. Fathers of the English Dominican Province (New York: Benzinger Bros., 1948), 363-382.

In the poem "Odysseus," written in honor of Winters, Finlay describes the hero of the ancient epic at sea, battered by the tumult of nature. Odysseus is the good man as Winters often described him: willing to essay the dangers of nature but with the moral fortitude to resist succumbing to its power. Odysseus wakes from a dream about his long voyage to find himself safe, at home in Ithaca. He rises and goes outside, where he

> Stared down slopes below encrusted walls
> Whose stone absorbed the cries of closing surf.
> From where I stood I saw, at its low edge,
> The narrow beach that, momently submerged,
> Withstood the wide explosions of the tide.[42]

The plain, almost prosaic, blank verse of these lines is typical of Finlay's work, which is mostly in iambic pentameter and usually blank rather than rhymed; it is also a quality he particularly learned from Winters. Winters was a defender of the "plain style."[43] He was also an advocate of what he called the "post-symbolist method," a practice of composition typical of modern literature in general and illustrated in this poem, where the meaning of the poem is conveyed primarily through a concrete description, rich with symbolic connotation, and presented largely without commentary.[44] Finlay here depicts the fortitude and stability

---

42. Finlay, *The Collected Poems*, 26.

43. Yvor Winters, *Forms of Discovery* (Chicago: The Swallow Press, 1967), 299-352.

44. Winters, *Forms of Discovery*, 251-298.

of Odysseus's soul, which has suffered much but not succumbed. He does so by describing the shore of Ithaca itself, which is "momently submerged" but nonetheless withstands the tide. The poem honors the rational toughness, as it were, of Winters's principles, but also represents nature after the fashion of Winters—as a menacing deluge.

"To a Victim of AIDS," a poem in which Finlay implicitly addresses himself and which was published just as the symptoms of the disease that would kill him had become unconcealable, focuses on what happens to one who refuses any rational government of his desires. Those desires "Destroyed the man that you had been," he writes, before noting that "You scorned judgment," that is to say, any moral rule superior to the impulse of sex, as "pure tyranny."[45] The conclusion bears an uncanny resemblance to the malevolent invasions described by Winters in his poems and criticism:

> Your body became your state of soul.
> It can't condemn one thing, but must
> Permit what comes, with no control.
> The germ not killed now breeds in lust
> On its own self, and kills the whole.[46]

His soul was wounded by sin, and now the disease acquired through sin becomes the "state" of the body. Matter is passive and subject to the formal activity of the soul;

---

45. Finlay, *The Collected Poems*, 60.

46. Finlay, *The Collected Poems*, 60.

so now the body is defenseless against the disease, which is of the flesh, and pullulates in the flesh, but is destructive of it as well. The "germ" of the virus, which was contracted through a specifically sterile form of lust, now proves fatefully capable of breeding. As it replicates itself it kills "the whole"—the composite body and soul of the one man.

Jeffrey Goodman once described Finlay's as the finest poem written about the AIDS crisis, which was a very large claim given that an older disciple of Winters, the poet Thom Gunn, received awards and extensive critical recognition for his depiction of the crisis in San Francisco, in his book *The Man with Night Sweats*.[47] Finlay's poem's first cinquain stanza is historically important insofar as it shows the fear and uncertainty regarding how the virus was spread in the 1980s. Its second stanza is the one moment in all of Finlay's poetry where he represents—in the diction of the milieu—a scene from his secret life. But it is this final stanza that matters most, for it shows the way the sin of the flesh that overcame his soul would, in turn, consume his flesh—and this is a death of "the whole." Finlay describes the genuine composite unity of body and soul and diagnoses the failure of the mind to govern properly the urges of the blood.

Finlay judges the AIDS virus as a deadly consequence of the rational soul's failure to govern the body. He does not propose denying the claims of the body but rather

---

47. Jeffrey Goodman, "*Mind and Blood:* An Introduction to the Poetry of John Finlay," in *In Light Apart: The Achievement of John Finlay*, ed. David Middleton (Glenside, PA: The Aldine Press, Inc., 1999), 30.

putting them in right order. His poem in tribute to Winters suggests the necessity of the strong rock of reason. In other poems he gives us a sense not only of the discipline of reason but the goodness of being and the measure of a life well lived. In "The Fourth Watch," Finlay meditates, in sesta rima stanzas, upon the nature and purpose of Christ's incarnation as our means of salvation. The poem begins in the viscera of the world, where the fisherman Peter is conscious of the foam of the sea, the "guts of fish," the "sod" of the earth. The first stanza concludes,

> In light apart from me, I seek the Word
> Holding mind and blood from the absurd.[48]

This short verse indicates two of Finlay's concerns. First, the "light" of the divine mind must be "apart" from the creature; we are not our own end, but must seek an end that transcends us, and this end will be the *Logos*, the Word, whose reason causes the world to be and orders the structure of reality. Our good as creatures is to be conformed to it. Second, the redemption made possible in that conformity is of "mind and blood" both; it is a redemption of soul and body together. If salvation lies in the *Logos*, the divine intellect, then sin and destruction are its opposite—they are the absurdity into which the creature's will might drive itself. They are not alternatives to reason but merely its negation.

The poem describes the human person as a composite whole. "You made us out of nothing, primal Word,"

---

48. Finlay, *The Collected Poems*, 24.

it professes. What is the relationship between the Incarnate Word and the human creature? The stanza continues, "My essence is not You by matter blurred."[49] Here, Finlay rejects an idea he first encountered in Winters's poem, "To the Holy Spirit." In that poem, Winters shows his existential neutrality by acknowledging the likeness of the human mind to the divine mind and yet attributing to the body nothing but its fallen mortality. On Winters's scheme, the body "blurs" or merely obscures the disembodied, divine and rational truth of the soul. Finlay insists on the opposite: the hypostatic union that draws divine and human natures into the single person of Christ does not conceal God but, on the contrary, reveals him to us more fully. We sense all the more the dependence of our embodied existence on the one who made us: "I am because of You."[50] If Christ causes our existence, body and soul, so also does his incarnation and paschal sacrifice save us entire, not merely our souls. Christ takes on flesh to save mind and blood alike, as the final stanza impressively explores:

> Embedded mind sustains the complex whole
> Redeemed with blood of Deity made flesh—
> You save the man, not disembodied soul.
> And summer burns the tireless sun afresh:
> A wedding-feast out under shade of limes,
> The servants brimming water-jars with wine![51]

---

49. Finlay, *The Collected Poems*, 24.

50. Finlay, *The Collected Poems*, 24.

51. Finlay, *The Collected Poems*, 25.

Here at last is the vision of the world Finlay would affirm against the tragic and stoic vision of Winters. Christ's incarnation vouches for the value of the flesh; he would not condemn the blood but redeem it with his own. The world itself, redeemed by Christ, is a new creation, indeed a new Cana: a "wedding-feast" "brimming" with miraculous jars of wine.

In "A Prayer to the Paraclete," a poem which follows closely Winters's "To the Holy Spirit," while also contradicting it, Finlay emphasizes that the Holy Spirit inspires "Our soul's and body's life," healing the "fractured, wounded will," and does so through the Eucharist: "Christ gives us God to share / In His shed blood as man."[52] The poem's four stanzas give priority to the coming-to-perfection of the "barren mind" and the poem turns to the will only secondarily, as we would expect to find in Winters, but the distinctive emphasis of the first and final stanzas is on the hypostatic union of Christ as at once God and man and to the composite wholeness of the human being as flesh and blood. The hypostatic union and the composite, hylomorphic, nature of the human person are separate concepts, but both insist upon the fullness, the goodness, and the dignity of that which is incarnate.

Finlay's vision of rational self-mastery and redemption in Christ wedded to the goodness of created being finds its most placid expression in "The Autobiography of a Benedictine." There, the Benedictine has all the admirable features that Finlay would have liked for himself. He

---

52. Finlay, *The Collected Poems,* 71.

is a scholastic who teaches logic and can "track down fallacies of fools."[53] He is humanistic, reading "dry Horace" while he drinks "wine deep," but with a moderation that will never "drown my wits."[54] He does not argue for, but merely adores, the reality of the Incarnation:

> I feel at ease here on this earth
> And love the dogma of God's flesh.[55]

Those who do otherwise, and reject the flesh like "eunuchs" or reject reason like romantics, he simply "leave[s] alone."[56] And he envisions our journey to God not as the disembodied Hades of Virgil, but as faith's death, when the fullness of the being of the vision of "the deathless Word" becomes the fulfillment of our being, body and soul as one.[57] This was the vision of existence Finlay admired and sought, but which proved elusive because of the "demon" possessing him. Winters helped him to frame that vision, however imperfectly. As we shall see, while that vision found expression in a number of his poems, it would find its most perfect expression even as he was breathing his last breaths and dictating his final poem to his sister.

---

53. Finlay, *The Collected Poems,* 73.

54. Finlay, *The Collected Poems,* 73.

55. Finlay, *The Collected Poems,* 73.

56. Finlay, *The Collected Poems,* 73.

57. Finlay, *The Collected Poems,* 73.

Tate's influence on Finlay's work was as pervasive as that of Winters. I will attend to the two most conspicuous aspects of it here. First, to Tate's theory of the modern age as gnostic and so at war with itself and, second, to Tate's role in fostering the "lean language" of southern poetry, a language that Finlay would cultivate to express the internecine violence of the Civil War, in particular, and southern culture more generally.

The late lecture of Tate's that I mentioned above, "Mere Literature and the Lost Traveller," is in one very good sense a valedictory work. It draws together in especially clear terms three ideas with which Tate had been concerned throughout his career. The first, and central, idea is what C. P. Snow described as the contest of the "two cultures," science and the humanities, in modern western intellectual life. Tate, along with his fellow Fugitive, Agrarian, and New Critical writers, had long argued that the culture of the sciences was a totalizing project that would conquer the world only by stripping away and denying the reality of whatever did not fit into the paradigm of the physical sciences. The realm of value or quality was the first to go. While the experimental physical sciences posed a significant threat, it was the "behavioral sciences" that were most dangerous.[58] Modern chemistry merely replaced earlier theories of matter and tempted us, with its experimental successes, to think it might be the only way to achieve certain knowledge. But the behavioral sciences,

---

58. Tate, "Mere Literature and the Lost Traveller," 93.

such as psychology and sociology, sought to replace the wisdom of metaphysics and ethics with an empirical, purely materialist account of "behavior." It was here that science most aggressively encroached on the terrain of the humanities.

In the lecture, Tate cites Aristotle's *Nicomachean Ethics*, where the philosopher argues that each field of study must seek only that level of precision that is appropriate to the subject. Agreeing with this, Tate argues that Aristotle "seemed to know a social science is impossible."[59] This is not, in fact, the case. Everything Aristotle discussed in his corpus was a science as he understood that term, that is to say, it was a study of causes. Science is the knowledge of causes, and we may have more or less precise knowledge of them, depending on the relative composition of necessary and contingent elements in the subject.[60] According to Tate, however, only exact knowledge constituted science, and so everything that transcended its empirico-mathematical methods could not be known scientifically or classified as science. Such things could, however, be known through literature and religion, neither of which were sciences, but both of which were transcendent ways of knowing.[61] This conclusion helps explain Tate's best-known concerns: his agrarian arguments in favor of the culture of the South and

59. Tate, "Mere Literature and the Lost Traveller," 94.

60. Aristotle, *Analytica Posteriora* 71b.8-12 in *The Basic Works of Aristotle*, ed. Richard McKeon (New York: Modern Library 2001).

61. Tate, "Mere Literature and the Lost Traveller," 94.

his New Critical arguments in favor of the study of poetic form. In the former, traditional cultural life, independent of scientific reasoning, fostered religious life and made humane value possible. In the latter, artistic form—the realm of quality—provided a specifically non-scientific means of knowing the world. This account of religion and literature constitutes Tate's second long-pursued argument.

In the context of this contest between science, on the one hand, and literature and religion on the other, Tate introduces a third note in the lecture—one to be found implicit in his earlier writing but made explicit only here. He draws on the celebrated work of the philosophers Eric Voegelin and Hans Jonas to propose that modern poetry has followed the experimental sciences in one way: it has elevated poetry to "a kind of Gnosis, accessible to the few who were lucky enough to be among the Elect."[62] He contrasts the orthodox Christian understanding of the "theological virtues" as everyone's means of salvation with the gnostic claim that a secret knowledge will save the few.[63] That secret knowledge splits the world in two, argues Tate. It claims "the natural world is beyond redemption, for it was created by the powers of evil" and the gnostic Christ "gives us the central mythical figure for this alienation of man from God and nature."[64] For Tate, gnosticism was the modern scientific project reconceived as an

---

62. Tate, "Mere Literature and the Lost Traveller," 96.

63. Tate, "Mere Literature and the Lost Traveller," 96.

64. Tate, "Mere Literature and the Lost Traveller," 97.

esoteric spiritual religion. It stripped away the richness of the world not by reducing it, by certain and experimental method, to matter but by dismissing matter as evil; and, further, it re-described salvation as a secret exact knowledge, as opposed to the freely given wisdom of faith offered by orthodox Christianity. On this scheme, poetry could be a form of gnostic knowledge, but only insofar as Hart Crane and other modernists rejected inherited wisdom and tradition in favor of "Doorways and world-structures beyond the common reach."[65]

Finlay was much impressed by these final words of Tate's. They spoke to his conviction that the true account of the world was the one that justified his admiration for those "good Thomistic animals," the cows; that is to say, natural being was good in itself, while sin and evil were mere defects of the good rather than realities unto themselves. He rejected Manichean dualism in favor of the divisible but finally unified order of Aquinas. Tate's briefly formulated theory of gnosticism, fruitful in itself, also caused a problem. Once one defined gnosticism in such a loose way, it became easy to see versions of it hidden just about everywhere in modernity or, as it happens, simply everywhere. Indeed, while Tate's account of gnosticism helped Finlay to define his differences with Winters more justly than he might otherwise have done, it also would give shape to Finlay's account of civilization in both his essays and his poems to such an extent that no small portion of his work consists of sniffing out gnostic heresies. He came

---

65. Tate, "Mere Literature and the Lost Traveller," 96.

to do so in such a manner that it seemed to infect nearly everything that was not clearly and explicitly as contentedly Thomist as the barnyard cows. Gnosticism became the blanket term of condemnation for anything that was not Aquinas as Finlay understood him. Gnosticism indeed was everywhere.

This criticism is most apt in regard to Finlay's one finished book of essays, *Flaubert in Egypt and Other Essays*. Each essay shows Finlay's lithe narrative style of criticism, leading us through the interior workings of a different figure's life. The essays as a whole indicate that, while he follows Tate in drawing on Hans Jonas's classic *The Gnostic Religion* to define gnosticism as a doctrine proclaiming "an ontological alienation of God from both the natural and human world," this is not a definition sufficiently rigorous to give the volume a compelling coherence. After Finlay's death, the poet and critic Helen Pinkerton would make a strong case that Finlay's argument was in line with the arguments of Jonas and Voegelin, and was more or less a just one.[66] Gerald Hartnett, in contrast, would find Finlay's use of the term "Gnosticism" ahistorical and, further, would judge Finlay's account of Aquinas to be narrow, rationalist, and more clearly derived from Aristotle than from the scholastic theologian.[67] Both critics were correct; what frustrates the reader of the volume is its gradual drift in argument, as "Gnosticism" becomes the diagnosis for a

---

66. Helen P. Trimpi, "Finlay on Winters's 'To the Holy Spirit,'" in *In Light Apart*, 136-151.

67. Gerald Hartnett, "Finlay's Thomism," in *In Light Apart*, 100-107.

range of philosophical convictions, some malodorous and some merely inferior to Aquinas's.

I have already summarized Finlay's chapter on Winters. The other four chapters in the volume can be discussed with similar brevity. In the title essay, Finlay proposes that Flaubert's alienation from the flesh, nature, sexuality, and even existence itself leads him to make a kind of mysticism of the aesthetic. The work of art becomes a sacred good apart from nature, characterized by form rather than content; thus it is enlisted as a substitute for God, and so the veneration of pure form becomes a worship of "nothingness."[68] Art becomes private cult and nihilism at once. His discussion of Paul Valéry runs along similar lines. Valéry's abiding influence in reflecting on the act of the creative mind in process is described as an "egoistic mysticism" that views the first act of creation, God's creation of nature, as itself a fall.[69] Pure creativity is good, but reification, which brings the creative act to an end, is bad. For Flaubert and Valéry everything outside the cult of the artist is a kind of "pollution."[70] Finlay's remarks are persuasive but not terribly surprising, given that modernism's esoteric and absolutist understanding of the aesthetic often put it in tension with nature and the divine. His two subjects, however, made a particular fetish of the artwork as a thing characterized by its alienation from the rest of creation. His argument that just such a contest between the little

---

68. Finlay, *The Collected Prose*, 41.

69. Finlay, *The Collected Prose*, 97, 95.

70. Finlay, *The Collected Prose*, 97.

god of art or ego and the true God of revelation repeats itself in the gnosticisms of Nietzsche, Freud, and Kafka is similarly sound and at times movingly articulated. The modern gnostics try again and again to kill God the father.

What remains most striking and intriguing about the volume is Finlay's revisionist account of two familiar Catholic figures of modern letters, John Henry Newman and Gerard Manley Hopkins. Finlay's point of departure in discussing Newman is the great convert's conviction that "the human intellect . . . is 'actually and historically' hostile to the operations of God's grace."[71] To explain and critique this conviction becomes Finlay's task; in doing so he delivers a crucial insight into Newman but does so in a manner that is insensitive to the details of intellectual history. Newman, he rightly observes, could only have perceived the intellect as hostile to religious belief if he took Enlightenment rationalism, from Locke and Hume to Mill, as descriptive of the intellect per se. And this, in a sense, Newman did. Indeed, a common way of understanding Newman's extended series of reflections on the nature of knowledge and belief is that he deliberately starts with the psychology of Locke and attempts to broaden it sufficiently to defend and preserve the reasonableness of Christian faith. For lack of a clear alternative, Newman grants modern assumptions and then tries to lead them back to orthodoxy.

Finlay argues that such a project was doomed from the start and is unnecessary. Enlightenment rationalism did not provide a true account of the nature of reason. It was in

---

71. Finlay, *The Collected Prose*, 44.

fact essentially anti-intellectual, with its various accounts of sense experience, instinct, association, and psychology each walling off the intellect from truth in a different theoretical manner. Authentic intellectualism leads by "logical inevitability" to "theism."[72] From Plato and Aristotle to the doctors of the Church, that the mind could know universal truths, separate from sensation and unconditioned by sensation, entailed also that one could know real ideas and the cause of all things, which is God. Newman's remaining within the ambit of Enlightenment reason and his failure to embrace the more venerable realism and intellectualism of the Church were signs that, despite his conversion, Newman remained a "Protestant" of the mind.[73] More damningly, Finlay contends,

> Newman brought into the Catholic Church this strain of Protestant anti-intellectualism, and I do not think his northern eyes ever accustomed themselves to the rational clarities of Aristotle and Aquinas. Assenting completely and sincerely to its theological dogma, he nevertheless fretted under the philosophical tradition of his adoptive church.[74]

---

72. Finlay, *The Collected Prose*, 63.

73. Finlay, *The Collected Prose*, 71.

74. Finlay, *The Collected Prose*, 71.

Here is where Finlay's history lacks sensitivity. Newman praised Aristotle in the highest terms, though his understanding of the philosopher was probably one corrupted by the theory of moral sentiments of the Scottish Enlightenment.[75] And so, here, Finlay has a point: Newman's Aristotle was probably not the real thing and was beholden to modern rationalism in its understanding of the Philosopher. But, after his conversion in 1845, Newman visited Rome and was disappointed to find a general depreciation and ignorance of Aristotle and Aquinas both.[76] That would change by the end of his lifetime,

75. Newman writes, "While the world lasts, will Aristotle's doctrine on these matters last, for he is the oracle of nature and truth. While we are men, we cannot help, to a great extent, being Aristotelians" (John Henry Newman, *The Idea of a University* (Notre Dame, IN: University of Notre Dame Press, 2013), 82-83. On the Scottish Enlightenment's misinterpretation and appropriation of Aristotle see—a text Finlay cites—Alasdair MacIntyre, *Whose Justice? Which Rationality?* (Notre Dame, IN: University of Notre Dame Press, 1985), 209-240. MacIntyre describes the figures of the Enlightenment as thinking themselves Aristotelians insofar as they shared roughly his table of moral virtues, but as to the origin and nature of what virtue was they were radically separated: Aristotle was an intellectualist, for whom moral virtues are reason's habitual government of the life of the body, whereas modern theories originate the whole moral life in the "sentiments" or passions. Newman had a similarly modern understanding of the nature of virtue.

76. Ernest L. Fortin, "'Sacred and Inviolable': *Rerum Novarum* and Natural Rights," *Theological Studies* 58 (1992): 230.

as the revival of Thomas Aquinas began to take hold in the Church, but that was a long, slow, and uneven process and one which endured for mere decades rather than centuries. *Aeterni Patris*, which for a time seemed to establish Aquinas as the sole philosopher of the Church, was promulgated in 1879. During most of Newman's career, therefore, other Catholic theologians were in no better a position to think with the intellectualism of Aquinas than was the early Newman. Like him, they were left to assemble new philosophical systems in response to the inadequacies of the towering modern figures of British empiricism, Cartesian rationalism, and German idealism.[77] The Aquinas with whom Finlay rightly and favorably contrasts Newman's thought was not really on the menu anywhere in Newman's day. There simply was no unified Catholic philosophy of a kind that might make him "fret." Newman admired from a distance Joseph de Maistre's traditionalist thought, while, some Continental Catholic philosophies of the day most likely unknown to Newman, such as the "ontologism" of Antonio Rosmini, advanced ideas very similar to Newman's.

Finlay was himself the beneficiary of the Thomistic revival, but his version of Aquinas is somewhat simplistic and distorts a key feature of Aquinas's thought. As we noted above, Finlay's Aquinas was a jolly rationalist who embraced the goodness of being, including the flesh. He was the Dumb Ox who loved cows, as it were, and this

---

77. Gerald A. McCool, S.J., *Nineteenth Century Scholasticism: The Search for a Unitary Method* (New York: Fordham University Press, 1989).

much is surely correct. But while Finlay's Thomism gives a generous respect to natural reason and being, it dismisses every trace of mysticism—including that found in Newman—as a symptom of anti-intellectualism and a basis for the charge of gnosticism.[78] In consequence, the range of natural discursive reason (*ratio*)—which excludes the intellectual basis (*intellectus*) of most Catholic mystical theology—gets unduly enlarged and mistaken for the whole of the intellect and this leaves a figure such as Newman looking like more of an outlier than he really was. While gnosticism is a heresy, there is inevitably a *gnosis* at the heart of Christianity and, in its highest forms of contemplation, even, as Hans Urs von Balthasar has noted, a certain "esoterism."[79] For Finlay, every hint of Platonism was a sign gnosticism would soon descend; for the actual Aquinas, Platonism indirectly but richly informed his thinking not only through the influence of Aristotle, but also that of Augustine and Dionysius the Aeropagite.

Something similar happens in Finlay's study of Hopkins. There, Hopkins's decision to destroy the poems he had written and to give up poetry in general so as to commit himself totally to Christ is taken to be a sign that the Puritan and romantic dimensions of his personality have overruled the Catholic.[80] Finlay makes a reasonable

---

78. Finlay, *The Collected Prose*, 68. See Middleton, *In Light Apart*, 102.

79. Hans Urs von Balthasar, *The Glory of the Lord*, trans. Erasmo Leiva-Merikakis (San Francisco: Ignatius Press, 1998) 1.33.

80. Finlay, *The Collected Prose*, 80.

point that this may suggest Hopkins's failure to accept the Thomistic vision of supernatural grace as completing nature rather than destroying it. Why else would Hopkins need to destroy his "secular" poems? Finlay also contends that Hopkins denies the traditional understanding of the unity of the human will as governing body and soul, but he pushes the argument so far that it comes to seem as though all theological traditions in the Church, including the Augustinian, per se lead to a voluntarist gnosticism. In this, he may have been following Winters, but that is no sign that the accusation is just.[81] This, in the end, leads him to describe Hopkins in a manner which may or may not be cogent in regard to the Victorian poet but which paints a vivid portrait of Finlay's own wrestling with his demon:

> Hopkins . . . split himself apart and waged systematic warfare in a divided will.

> But Hopkins discovered his helplessness in the presence of his own nature. The more he turned the screws of discipline, the more the pressure released the irrational raw powers of a nature that fought back like a cunning beast and drove him into states of madness.[82]

---

81. Winters, *In Defense of Reason*, 377.
82. Finlay, *The Collected Prose*, 76.

Finlay explicitly connects this gnostic madness with Hopkins's possible homosexuality.[83] If Finlay's Thomism is narrow and textbook, his understanding of history equally so, and his idea of gnosticism ahistorical and overly broad, one nonetheless senses the essays as driving toward a coherent vision of the world. Finlay wanted a philosophical vision that could hold together a judicious understanding of the natural reason as capable of attaining to being and the knowledge of God along with a warm embrace of the goodness of created being as itself ordered to God. The temptations to stray from that vision lay immanent in his soul. The modern heresies against it were many. So also, it turned out, were the ancient ones. In his last few working years, Finlay drafted three impressive essays on Plato and Platonism. "The Night of Alcibiades" is a familiar and yet riveting account of the relationship between Socrates and the tragic and traitorous Greek hero. "The Socratics and the Flight from This World" effectively traces gnosticism back to the world-retiring developments within neo-Platonic thought that were long before described as "the failure of nerve."[84] Neo-Platonism did indeed provide the philosophical structure for later varieties of gnosticism, but once again the phenomena Finlay tries to group under that term are so multitudinous and varied in detail that his effort does not prove very clarifying.

---

83. Finlay, *The Collected Prose*, 88.

84. Gilbert Murray, *Five Stages of Greek Religion* (New York: Columbia University Press, 1925). Murray's account has been influential but it is also tendentious and reductive.

Finlay's criticism, nonetheless, lays the groundwork for his poetry's attempt to critique the destructive flight from being of modern art and thought even as his poems also seek to reaffirm the goodness of natural being. The gnosticism of modern literature is detailed in a small group of poems including "The Faun," "The *Illumination of Arthur Rimbaud*," "Baudelaire in Belgium," and "Flaubert in Egypt." The central concern of these poems is expressed in two lines from the Rimbaud lyric:

> He gazed into its objectless pure style,
> Hermetic light destroying common earth[85]

The modernist practice of making the work of art a kind of autonomous, in some sense religious, absolute, even as it is reduced to pure form, in effect leads the modern artist to worship a god of the void, a formal nothingness. It is an artificial god, no less, and one that is hermetic (part of a secret *gnosis* brought about by the artist's intuition) and thus is alienating from, and destructive of, the goodness of natural being, that "common earth." "Flaubert" and "The Faun" both suggest that this gnostic tendency is a consequence of disordered desire and shame at recollected sin, "The half-forgotten wreckage" and "buried images" in the mind "Of women he had forced or gulled into / The brief and awkward void of his lust."[86] The modern artist

---

85. Finlay, *The Collected Poems*, 86.
86. Finlay, *The Collected Poems*, 83.

misuses the world, as a desired but worthless thing, and misattributes to the contingent little world of the art-work an absolute value.

Perhaps Finlay's best poem of this kind is "A Portrait of a Modern Artist." Its setting is contemporary and so the poem feels less like a study of literary history than do the others in this group. Furthermore, the psychology of the poem is more perceptive. Awake, the woman artist "writes hard fiction" whose "characters burn out on sex and drugs"; she is a novelist of the Brett Easton Ellis mold who provides a "clinical" depiction of "A world of sex and death shot up on coke."[87] In her sleep, however, human nature reasserts itself and a desire for more than the grind of flesh on flesh, a desire for "form and being" appears.[88] Most poems of such a darkly critical vein, including the others just mentioned, simply paint a damning portrait and leave the reader to make the final judgment.[89] The "Portrait" is distinctive in giving us a character with sufficient depth that she can at least glimpse "her disowned humanity."[90]

---

87. Finlay, *The Collected Poems*, 90.

88. Finlay, *The Collected Poems*, 90.

89. See, for instance, Yvor Winters's similar critiques of the modern poet, "Orpheus" and "Midas" (Yvor Winters, *Collected Poems* (Denver, CO: Alan Swallow, 1960), 79, 84) or his student Helen Pinkerton's "Subjectivity" and "Error Pursued" (Helen Pinkerton, *A Journey of the Mind* (Newburg, OR: Wiseblood Books, 2016), 24, 38-39). These and many other poems of the Winters circle are critical and yet reticent; they allow the error examined to appear as its own condemnation.

90. Finlay, *The Collected Poems*, 90.

In poem and essay alike, Finlay followed Tate's late critique of modern gnosticism. The results were mixed. Finlay was a perceptive critic of the weaknesses of the modern age and of modern artists, but he tended to reduce those weaknesses to a single common plague. That theory became more and more unfocused as apparent instances of it multiplied across the modern literary tradition and then cropped up in ancient Athens as well. Tate most profitably influenced Finlay, however, through another of his late works, this time a poem rather than an essay.

Although many of Tate's poems take the South for subject matter, most of them are dense and obscure lyrics of meditation, the best known of which is "Ode to the Confederate Dead." The poem, as Tate himself explained, is set within the psyche of a solitary figure whose typically modern problem is "solipsism," and this is typical of his work insofar as his chief concern was the dilemma of the modern person trapped within his own subjectivity.[91]

Among his last and greatest poems, however, is one very different from the rest. "The Swimmers," one of a series of poems written in terza rima, is unique in Tate's work in that it is, in appearance, a direct and literal narrative poem depicting an event from early in the poet's life: his witnessing of a lynching. While the poem, like all Tate's poems, is densely symbolic and obscure of syntax, it is nonetheless his plainest and most powerful. Although Finlay never discussed the poem in his published work, it clearly served as one of the models for Finlay's own poems

---

91. Allen Tate, *Essays of Four Decades* (Wilmington, DE: ISI Books, 1999), 595.

about the South. Finlay's poetry was most obviously influenced by the plain style and post-symbolist work of Winters, but Tate's poem has a similar restraint and, more importantly, exemplifies a poetry of the South that specifically addresses the violent tensions endemic to southern history by retelling that history. Winters wrote several restrained narrative poems, most in couplets, some in blank verse. Tate wrote only "The Swimmers," but it clearly did as much as Winters to help Finlay discover a means of representing the historical experience of the South.

Among the plain style lyrics Finlay published, an early one titled "The Wide Porch" serves as an *ars poetica* and hints that Finlay's career will be an exploration of the lost and ruined culture of the Deep South. His best poems generally do take the South, especially its tragic aspects, for subject. "The Dead and the Season," an elegy for his uncle, Duncan Finlay, who died in a farming accident, is among them. Its description of the silence of the house after his death in the hospital, which concludes the poem, is especially fine:

> We lived the remnant of that morning blurred:
> The chilled and silent house, engulfing light,
> Some neighbors who had come to cook our meal,
> The slugs of scalding whiskey for our blood.[92]

The poem that follows, "The Road to the Gulf," is even better, and in fact would be Finlay's best lyric but for a somewhat clumsy ending. The most obvious influence

92. Finlay, *The Collected Poems*, 50.

in the poem is not Tate but Winters, whose great poems in heroic couplets, especially "A View of Pasadena from the Hills" and "The Slow Pacific Swell," are echoed in form and style by Finlay. The first half of the poem runs as follows:

> A small white town, its silver water-tank
> Gleaming above a green deep river's bank,
> We passed before the pasture still unmowed
> And melons piled for sale beside the road.
> Samples were cut on shells of oyster blue,
> So ripe the seedless heart had split in two.
> The closer to the Gulf we came the more
> The flattened earth recalled itself as shore.[93]

The use of language here deliberately echoes Winters, especially the unusual use of the verb "recalled" in the last line, which creates a subtle analogy between the structure of the landscape and the structure of the human psyche. Finlay's description of the literal detail of the southern landscape is perceptive and extended here in a way it seldom was elsewhere. It is typical of him to move swiftly from the composition of place to abstract reflection (as he does in "At the Spanish Fort Near the Pensacola Naval Station") but here he remains merely in the descriptive mode, and the poem is the stronger for it. Other Finlay poems in couplets approach this one in quality, and I wish he had lived long enough to write more of this kind.

---

93. Finlay, *The Collected Poems*, 51.

Among his best poems is a series of short and mid-length narrative poems. Some of them he later collected as *The American Tragedies: A Chronology of Six Poems*, which he sent as a gift to the widow of Winters, Janet Lewis; another poem, "The Exiles," was not included in the sequence but was dedicated to Janet Lewis. All the poems retell episodes from the nineteenth century, from the time of the first encounters of white pioneers with American Indians, through their expulsion, and on to the time of the Civil War. Lewis, who was best known as a historical novelist and who sometimes wrote about Native Americans was a natural audience for these poems. She and Winters alike had drawn inspiration from Native American art and poetry. Finlay's choice of scenarios is often inventive; his verse is his normal blank verse, plainer than the plain style of Winters and deliberately prosaic.

"A Memory of the Frontier" describes the death of an old man and the preparation of his body by an "old slave woman."[94] Finlay's narrative and language are so expertly restrained that we can sense tension, grief, and horror throughout the poem and yet it is never allowed to break open, even in the closing, austere lines:

> They took the sheets
> Outside and burnt them in the evening fog—
> Fire struggled on the clamminess of blood.
> The man had had the coffin done by dark.
> The neighbors came; huddled at the hearth,
> We held a wake, then buried him by noon.[95]

---

94. Finlay, *The Collected Poems*, 69.

95. Finlay, *The Collected Poems*, 69.

These lines show Finlay taking possession of the narrative verse of Winters, as exemplified in "Sir Gawaine and the Green Knight" or in Winters's own "frontier" poem, "The Journey." The lines are muted but serious, in contrast to the mordant, almost cruel in its indifference, conclusion of Robert Frost's otherwise similar narrative of a death, "Out, Out—."

"The Pioneers" and "The Exiles" depict the first bloody conflicts between "The red men / and the whites."[96] The first of these poems is austere and even wooden in its narration. The second is more sinuous and divided into three parts, with each part entering more deeply into the interior of the narrator. In the first, conflict and expulsion are tersely described; in the second, a lost Indian woman with her papoose approaches a settler and he gives them food to eat; in the third, the memory of her persists within him: "For some time on the woman lived in me; / I followed her inside my taken mind."[97] "Told from the Nineteenth Century" is Faulknerian in its depiction of a pair of sisters ruined by "their father's blood, / Diseased by syphilis."[98] In similar fashion, "The Blood of Shiloh" retells the true story of a Finlay ancestor whose mind was ruined by his experience in battle. The portrait of his ancestor is sympathetic, in marked contrast to Finlay's treatment of his own infection of the blood. He understood human weakness but not for the purpose of excusing it in himself:

---

96. Finlay, *The Collected Poems*, 112.

97. Finlay, *The Collected Poems*, 113.

98. Finlay, *The Collected Poems*, 118.

I feel God's mercy found his godless mind.
He went mad not because a coarsened brain
In him craved evil, for he craved the good
Whose absence his good mind could not endure.[99]

The two most ambitious poems in the sequence are "Through a Glass Darkly" and especially "In the Time of Civil War." The first begins, "My uncle hated Catholics," but in the lines that follow we discover that he hated everyone, drunk or sober, and was himself an obese and monstrous caricature.[100] The poem is a portrait of his pain and wretchedness, but also his hapless desire for redemption, which finds expression only in his forcing his nephew to read him scripture aloud during his bouts of drink and sadness. The second, longer poem depicts the lynching of an Italian immigrant during the War; because of his dark skin, the neighbors suspect him of being a spy for the "Yankees."[101] He is, in fact, a romantic secular utopian of the Emerson variety, who has come to the United States to escape the Church: "He thought pure nature molded man to good / Freed from the old God, His kings and popes."[102] Even as he is being hanged he remains calm, as if still convinced of the romantic freedom and goodness of the new world of Alabama. The lynched man's wife, in contrast, is hysterical (her hysteria is well described by Finlay) and is also a faithful Catholic.

99. Finlay, *The Collected Poems*, 68.

100. Finlay, *The Collected Poems*, 119.

101. Finlay, *The Collected Poems*, 114.

102. Finlay, *The Collected Poems*, 115.

One of the most impressive moments in the poem occurs as the young narrator and his father escort her to Mobile, whence she will sail to Rome, leaving as a widow the frontier land onto which her husband had projected his naïve political ideology. In the big city, she sees a Catholic church, and the boy, to his father's discomfort, follows her into the "massive dimness of the church and gazed | As candles burned and lit the altar's gold."[103]

If "The Swimmers" is Tate's unique late accomplishment in narrative verse, so "In the Time of the Civil War" is Finlay's. It is the most complex, profound, and well-constructed of his narrative poems. The final scene's depiction of the young narrator following the woman into the Church ends without any sign of the experience having affected him: she "crossed herself in tears and turned away. | The next day she embarked and left for Rome."[104] But, in an earlier scene in the poem, we learn that the boy has been haunted by the lynched man. He has gone in search of his ghost:

> The town still says he haunts the water oaks.
> I went there one night seeking him, but found
> Just the pure moonlight falling in between
> The moving limbs; quick drops of it hit earth
> And ran like mercury on the black, hot ground.
> His ghost was wilderness, the burning moon.[105]

---

103. Finlay, *The Collected Poems*, 117.

104. Finlay, *The Collected Poems*, 117.

105. Finlay, *The Collected Poems*, 115.

Tate's poem sinks back into the historical memory of the South and describes it in compelling literal detail, but the lynched black man Tate depicts also moves beyond the literal, in the course of the poem, to serve as a figure of Christ. Naturally, it is not difficult for the poem to show us the connection between one scapegoat dead man and another, but Tate's poem nonetheless rattles a bit with the effort. In the passage just quoted, however, we see that Finlay has achieved a much subtler and more elegant symbolism. First, the boy goes in conscious quest of finding the risen ghost of the murdered utopian, the foiled secular messiah. We sense at once the power of the moment but also its failure: the boy recognizes that the place is haunted but not in the way he originally suspects. Then, at the conclusion of the poem, the boy enters the church with the widow, and while his emotional response to what he finds there is muted, the literal details quietly indicate that here, amid the "altar's gold," the real presence of a living body is to be found, even if the boy is too young to understand the "peace" and absolution experienced by the woman.[106] The two moments resonate with one another so that Finlay allows the narrator's emotion to show forth however slightly in the first one even as we see those feelings only find their answer in the second. It is a masterpiece of plot structure and of verse craft.

The sequence of "American Tragedies" shows Finlay's mature achievement and also his limitations. All of them were written in the last half-decade of his life and, though some are under-imagined and uninventive in language,

---

106. Finlay, *The Collected Poems*, 117.

some of them are impressive enough to leave us thinking it likely that his significance as a narrative poet would only have increased had he had more time and a wider, more critical readership, to help him to cultivate the form.

Two more poems that take the South for subject must be mentioned. "The Slaughter of the Herd" describes the end of the Finlay family's long practice of raising cattle. It appeared immediately following three of Finlay's "American Tragedies" historical narratives, and so the contrast between an older, more primitive southern life and the opening lines' presentation of commercial agriculture, even in its failing moment, is marked:

> The trucks will come tomorrow afternoon.
> The herd her family had milked for years
> Will then be prodded with electric shocks,
> Packed and crammed inside the storied trucks
> And driven to the auction ring for slaughter.[107]

Finlay's debt to Tate, the agrarian, becomes clear here. The agrarians had generally prized subsistence farming specifically because it allowed for a rich culture and stable way of life resistant to the forces of exchange, as Ransom had argued in his last, most detailed, and long lost agrarian treatise, *Land!*[108] The necessities of the modern farm in an industrial society, however, lead to a selling-off, a surrend-

---

107. Finlay, *The Collected Poems*, 121.

108. John Crowe Ransom, *Land!* (Notre Dame, IN: University of Notre Dame Press, 2017).

ering of the stability of place and the traditional patterns of life that stand outside the market and which Tate, Ransom, and others had wanted to defend. At the beginning of this essay, we took note of Finlay, on the family dairy farm, appreciating the "Thomistic" solidity of cattle. In this poem, they symbolize a whole way of life soon to be lost:

> She saw a world not man's in speechless calm.
> The cattle as they slept or grazed appeared
> Like creatures in some myth, whole and primal.
> Their bags hung heavy with the morning milk.[109]

A somewhat earlier poem, "Salt from the Winter Sea," is among Finlay's three or four best. Like the "American Tragedies" poems, it describes life in the Old South, specifically the practice of the farmers traveling to the Gulf to harvest sea salt in winter:

> Black pots boiled for days among the gulls
> Upon white dunes, sea-water steaming off
> And leaving salt. They sifted out the gross
> Impurities. In cool depths of hogsheads
> The fusing salt was stored away from heat.[110]

Most of Finlay's poems on the South describe either the violence of the past or the slow decline of a way of life, which was set in motion by that violence. Here, the

---

109. Finlay, *The Collected Poems*, 121.

110. Finlay, *The Collected Poems*, 75.

hard work of the farmers is depicted and the concern with survival would seem to consume their lives—and so it does, except for one moment of stillness, freedom, and contemplation:

> But the last day, after their work was done,
> Those stoics lingered in the cloudless calm,
> The warm November sun of their Deep South,
> The green Gulf crashing on the golden sand.
> They momently then gazed outside themselves,
> Struck by the mortal beauty of the waves,
> Before they packed the salt and started home.[111]

As we noted above, when Finlay uses the word "salt," it typically refers to wit and rational vision, those particular strengths, according to Winters's poetic theory. But here, salt becomes the natural symbol of aesthetic excess, of savor and satisfied fulfillment, those properties of being that are made possible by the reality of beauty. The poem is not perfect: "stoics" and "Deep South" seem crude and hasty substitutes for the kind of perceptive language worthy of the rest of this poem. The adverb of "momently" is not a blemish, but an allusion to Winters's own great meditative lyric on technology, necessity, and love, "At the San Francisco Airport."[112] But where Winters's poem ends in

---

111. Finlay, *The Collected Poems*, 75.

112. Winters writes, "The rain of matter upon sense / Destroys me momently. The score: / There comes what will come" (Winters, *Collected Poems*, 143).

a state of apprehension, Finlay's gives us awe and stillness even beneath the heavy yoke of labor. It gives us in a simple vision and as an experience the sought-for peace that "Autobiography of a Benedictine" merely describes.

To the Father

Finlay's Catholicism was shaped by his respect for the cool rational figures of Aquinas and Aristotle, specifically in their affirmation of the capacity of natural reason to know being and truth and to govern itself in conformity with reality. At the time of his conversion, Middleton tells us, Finlay seemed far more devoted to the knowledge of God than to the love of him.[113] His poems typically express his preference for "salt," for the dry wit of the clarified intellect, whereas, when the poems are emotionally pitched they are so in remorse for the "demon" that sometimes possessed that intellect and turned it to perverse ends. In this respect, Finlay may be compared to the great French symbolist poet Charles Baudelaire.

Baudelaire's book of poems, *Les Fleurs du Mal* (1857), depicted in verse the Parisian demi-monde with all its sordid figures. It judged sin for what it was, sin. Baudelaire was as certain of the reality of the devil as he was of God. What he could not bring himself to do, while he died of syphilis, was repent, and thus many of his poems speak of his own inexorable damnation. For some of the poets who followed him, Baudelaire was an inspiration to render in verse

---

113. Finlay, *The Collected Prose*, 366.

the seamy side of modern urban life, but for others he was a poet of disillusioned moral seriousness, and his vision moved them—as it could not move him—to repentance and into the Church.

Finlay contracted AIDS in the demi-monde of New Orleans. When he writes, "I leave now your dank underground small room / Where your lonely cold ego meets its doom," he is addressing the demon within him, but also Baudelaire who possessed those rooms before him.[114] He both desired the sensations of evil and was destroyed by them. But, as we noted, he was also a convert to the Catholic Church, his reception coming in the same year that he first suspected the presence of the disease that killed him. His early poems depict evil but, as we saw, do not glorify it; they rather reckon with the continuing temptation of the "demon." This is perhaps best demonstrated in an otherwise modest poem, "The Case of Holmes," where the rivalry between the famous detective and his nemesis Professor Moriarty becomes a symbol of Finlay's own erotic attraction to the enemy he wished to defeat:

> He has to drug a mind that will not cease
> Once a case is solved—cocaine's release,
> Or trance before the chemical blue flame.
> And there are states of mind he cannot name,
> As skulking in the fog, urban night-wood,
> He feels compressed, erotic brotherhood
> And for the hardest criminal.[115]

---

114. Finlay, *The Collected Poems*, 94.

115. Finlay, *The Collected Poems*, 38.

Several of Finlay's poems achieve tension precisely because they place us in that unsettled moment of "erotic brotherhood." Most of his best lyrics, however, speak most powerfully about the rational equipoise he long had sought, but which was only achieved during the long death sentence of his last decade. In both cases, the poems are in a sense fantasy: fantasy regarding the danger of what could—and would—become his ruin; fantasy regarding the tough Thomistic mind that could—and would—become his salvation.

As he lay in bed, in the living room of the family home, unable any longer to write or even to see, Finlay dictated his single best poem to his sister, "A Prayer to the Father." It is also a poem of fantasy, but with a crucial difference. There, Finlay is no longer dreaming of the demonic life he was tempted to indulge in nor of the rational life he struggled to attain. He has known the demon, but he has also overcome it. He has found peace in Christ. The only fantasy left to him, as he lies dying, is to envision the movement from the hearing of faith to the vision of God. "Death is not far from me," he begins,

> At times I crave
> The peace I think that it will bring. Be brave,
> I tell myself, for soon your pain will cease.[116]

The poem returns to the couplets of Winters that he had adopted in many of his poems, including "Holmes," "A Room for a Still Life," "Ovid in Exile," and that near-perfect

---

116. Finlay, *The Collected Poems*, 82.

masterpiece, "The Road to the Gulf." The brief, punctuated sentences and the enjambment across the first two lines gives the impression of plain speech rather than verse, the candor of interior reflection. Finlay would not live long enough to revise the poem much, and the next two lines contain two weaknesses, one of language (a cliché) and one of meter; but they lead us nonetheless to the Thomistic vision of the soul as the form of the body:

> But terror still obtains when our long lease
> On life ends at last. Body and soul,
> Which fused together should make up one whole,
> Suffer deprived as they are wrenched apart.[117]

We are composite beings. We are not our souls alone, but "one whole." The "lease," however, should have been qualified as "short," and the line that follows is missing an unstressed syllable before "ends." From the precipice of fear, Finlay's words now turn entirely to God, in petition that his suffering may be not merely ended but genuinely overcome and that his natural reason, which can only know God discursively by rational demonstration and the hearing of faith, may come to contemplate the light of the divine essence at last through the unmediated vision of the intellect:

> O God of love and power, hold still my heart
> When death, that ancient, awful fact appears;

---

117. Finlay, *The Collected Poems*, 82.

Preserve my mind from all deranging fears,
And let me offer up my reason free
And where I thought, there see Thee perfectly.[118]

The allusion to the last books of Augustine's *Confessions*, where the saint begs God to hold his heart steady so that he may understand the natures of time and eternity, is here rendered an expression of agony and a plea for mercy rather than curiosity.[119] The human flesh is weak and requires grace, divine aid, to accomplish its end, which is to know God. The final two lines speak of reason's transformation from a mere act of thinking ("where I thought") to one of perfect seeing. They are a stylistic and theological masterstroke. Aquinas's extended meditations, in the *Summa Contra Gentiles*, on perfect happiness and on the human good as nothing less than the contemplation of God are voiced in a simple offering of the poet's life to God.[120] All that the body suffers, all that the mind conceives, are for the sake of pure vision, where the intellect has nothing left to do but stand in joy and "drink."[121]

---

118. Finlay, *The Collected Poems*, 82.

119. Augustine of Hippo, *Confessions*, trans. Maria Boulding (Hyde Park, NY: New City Press, 1997), 11.

120. Saint Thomas Aquinas, *Summa Contra Gentiles*, trans. Vernon J. Bourke (Notre Dame, IN: University of Notre Dame Press, 2001), 3.25-41.

121. " . . . like a stag at the gushing spring, intelligence has nothing to do but drink; it drinks the clarity of being" (Jacques Maritain, *Art and Scholasticism and the Frontiers of Poetry*, trans. Joseph Evans (New York: Charles Scribner's Sons, 1962), 26).

Under the tutelage of Tate and Winters, Finlay was early able to discern style and subject matter worthy of making him a major poet. Although he had a lively literary circle during his years at LSU, most of the writing for which he will be remembered, in prose and verse, was written during that final decade of provincial isolation, incurable disease, and a torturous, slow death. This hurt the quality of his writing in at least two ways. The thesis guiding his essays on the gnostic element in literature is too generalized and too abstracted from the actual currents of intellectual history to be wholly insightful, even as the spirit and style of those pages are themselves exhilarating and remind one of the best criticism of Tate and Winters. Had he written them as part of a broader critical conversation, his arguments might have found greater refinement and subtlety.

Although Finlay sometimes exchanged poems with his fellow poet and future executor, Middleton, his ear for meter was an imperfect one. As Clive Wilmer once observed, Finlay's poems suffer from "garbled or bungled scansion," and indeed there is no poem that does not have at least one metrically flawed line.[122] As Wilmer also notes, Finlay's work in rhyme was generally inferior to his work in blank verse, with the exception of his occasional use of the Wintersian couplet.[123] In consequence, most of

---

122. Clive Wilmer, "John Finlay's *Mind and Blood*," in *In Light Apart*, 177.

123. Clive Wilmer, "John Finlay's *Mind and Blood*," in *In Light Apart*, 176. Middleton notes, "John was sometimes sloppy

Finlay's attempts at the epigram are forgettable. His strongest work is in blank verse, but here Finlay sometimes failed to modulate his syntax and he settled for lines that in some ways resemble those Timothy Steele describes as a structure "composed of two noun phrases connected by a monosyllabic conjunction or preposition," which quickly sounds redundant.[124] One hears four words weighing heavily and see-sawing across the middle of the iambic line, as in the opening of "The Pioneers":

> The white man aimed his rifle at the head
> And waited as the chief approached the house,
> Soundless on muffling needles of the pine.
> A band of young braves moved behind his back.[125]

No individual line is poor, but the structure as a whole is repetitive. We hear "white man" and "head," "chief" and "house," "needles" and "pine" and "braves" and "back," tipping back and forth in the syntax. He would have benefited from having many more occasions to read his poems aloud and to test them on the ear of another.

Finlay could also sometimes fall back on easy or trite expressions, such as the "white man" just quoted, or (as we noted above) the pat reference to the farmers at the gulf as

---

with meter, rhyme, line length along with syllable counting, filler words such as 'still' . . . and could even be obscure . . ." (*The Collected Prose*, 367).

124. Timothy Steele, *All the Fun's in How You Say a Thing* (Athens, OH: Ohio University Press, 1999), 152.

125. Finlay, *The Collected Poems,* 97.

"stoics." But he also fixed on inexpressive abstractions that refer to regions or national character, as in the phrase "of their Deep South," or "My Gallic cunning," which opens "Audubon at Oakley" and "Latin names" (which by itself is fine) and "Saxon salt," which end it.[126] He had a proclivity for the word "core" (which I surmise is a borrowing from Yeats) and, as we have noted, for "salt." The former never seems to work where he puts it, while the latter is essential to the themes of Finlay's poems but is nonetheless over-used. Its presence spoils his first important poem, "The Wide Porch," for instance. In that poem, all the imagery is of a southern farm landscape, and yet he refers to leaving the farm behind with a totally out of place simile: "A swimmer coming out of blinding salt."[127] The figure risks ruining the poem for the very small gain of using his favorite code word.

But Finlay did not live the life of the mind in vain. In the short lease on life he was given, as he stared for ten years at the approaching darkness of death, and felt it withering his body, part by part, he worked through his nights to make a number of memorable poems and to carry on the intellectual and critical legacies of Tate and Winters. He was a worthy, if doomed, successor, who made their thought his own.

In addition to the poems we have examined here, he wrote a number of others that in whole or in part merit the reader's attention. The fourth stanza of "The Wide Porch," for instance:

126. Finlay, *The Collected Poems,* 28.
127. Finlay, *The Collected Poems,* 14.

I swept away the clotted leaves and dirt
From graves my uncle took me out to clean.
The massive autumns drunk on their own seed,
Staining the chilled slabs, nothing underneath—
I then moved outward to become myself.[128]

The description of the victim in the third stanza of
"The Bog Sacrifice" is strong in an otherwise attenuated
lyric. "A Room for a Still Life" is a nearly perfect tableau
in couplets; but like "The Road to the Gulf" it is marred
by its closing lines. So also, in "Audubon at Oakley," the
description of one instance of the French illustrator's work
is evocative:

I saw my book, taut wings of mockingbirds
In combat with the snake knotted beneath
The nest, its open mouth close to the eggs,
Now held forever in the lean, hard line.[129]

In one of his last poems, "The Symposium for Socrates," we see that his essays in philosophy were a way
of entering more surely into the intellectual life as Finlay
understood it: "wisdom like salt / Which our own minds
can gather from the sea, / Shall be tonight the substance
of our talk."[130] Such lines, which echo many of his other
poems, make a fine coda to his work, even if they are not as
moving as that final poem, "A Prayer to the Father."

---

128. Finlay, *The Collected Poems*, 13.

129. Finlay, *The Collected Poems*, 28.

130. Finlay, *The Collected Poems*, 125.

In Finlay's lifetime, and in the decades following his death, talented poets, especially fellow disciples of Winters and Tate, recognized and paid tribute to his work, publishing poems and essays in his honor.[131] He is among the most important poets of the modern South and, like Tate before him, he remains one of our most compelling American Catholic poets. He entered more deeply into the Catholic tradition than did Tate, and the Church in one way or another gives form to all his work. He also exemplifies Winters's understanding of the poem as a technique of contemplation; writing verse was a means for him to appreciate the natural goodness of being, aiding him in disciplining the mind, while it helped him to understand the demon that tormented him and finally ended his life. Where Winters drew on Aquinas but held him at a distance, treating him as a philosophical master but not a religious one, Finlay embraced the scholastic theologian as wholly as he could and with passion. If Finlay's Thomism is a little wayward, it is so only because he was so anxious to communicate Aquinas's understanding of body and soul as a composite unity and to defend the natural goodness of being against every "Gnostic" heresy. Along with another Winters student also devoted to Aquinas, Helen Pinkerton, Finlay is practically the only contemporary writer to practice a genuinely metaphysical poetics. Dying young and largely unknown, Finlay was a minor talent of major ambition, whose work deserves to be remembered.

---

131. Including David Middleton, ed., *A Garland for John Finlay* (Thibodaux, LA: Blue Heron Press, 1990). The poems in this small chapbook were read aloud to Finlay during his final months.

ABOUT THE AUTHOR

James Matthew Wilson is the Cullen Foundation Chair in English Literature and the founding director of the MFA program in Creative Writing at the University of Saint Thomas. The author of fourteen books, his most recent collection of poems is *Saint Thomas and the Forbidden Birds* (Word on Fire, 2024). *The Strangeness of the Good* (2020), won the poetry book of the year award from the Catholic Media Awards. The Dallas Institute of Humanities awarded him the Hiett Prize in 2017; Memoria College gave him the Parnassus Prize, in 2022; and the Conference on Christianity and Literature twice gave him the Lionel Basney Award. In addition to his role at the University of Saint Thomas, he serves as poet-in-residence of the Benedict XVI Institute, scholar-in-residence of Aquinas College, editor of Colosseum Books, and poetry editor of *Modern Age* magazine.

Portions of this essay first appeared in *Catholic World Report, Notre Dame Church Life Journal,* and *The European Conservative.*

WISEBLOOD ESSAYS IN CONTEMPORARY CULTURE

Wiseblood Essays in Contemporary Culture offer in-depth interpretations of literature and art at large from a distinctly Catholic vantage point, while also championing and criticizing notable Catholic contributions to culture.

SELECTED TITLES

A Theology of Fiction
Cassandra Nelson

Jane Austen's Darkness
Julia Yost

The Catholic Writer Today
Dana Gioia

Christopher Beha: Novelist in a Postsecular World
Katy Carl

"Everything Came to Me at Once":
The Intellectual Vision of René Girard
Cynthia L. Haven

How to Think Like a Poet
Ryan Wilson

Duty, the Soul of Beauty:
Henry James on the Beautiful Life
R. R. Reno

The Tragedy of the Republic
Pierre Manent

Death Comes for the Cathedrals
Marcel Proust

Poetry and Mysticism
Raïssa Maritain

Christianity and Poetry
Dana Gioia

www.ingramcontent.com/pod-product-compliance
Lightning Source LLC
Chambersburg PA
CBHW071542120626
46550CB00006B/2545